To
Kinny & Joey;

Two special boys who
are loved. Enjoy both
this special look for both
of you.

Love, Leisha & Leo

This book belongs to:

_____

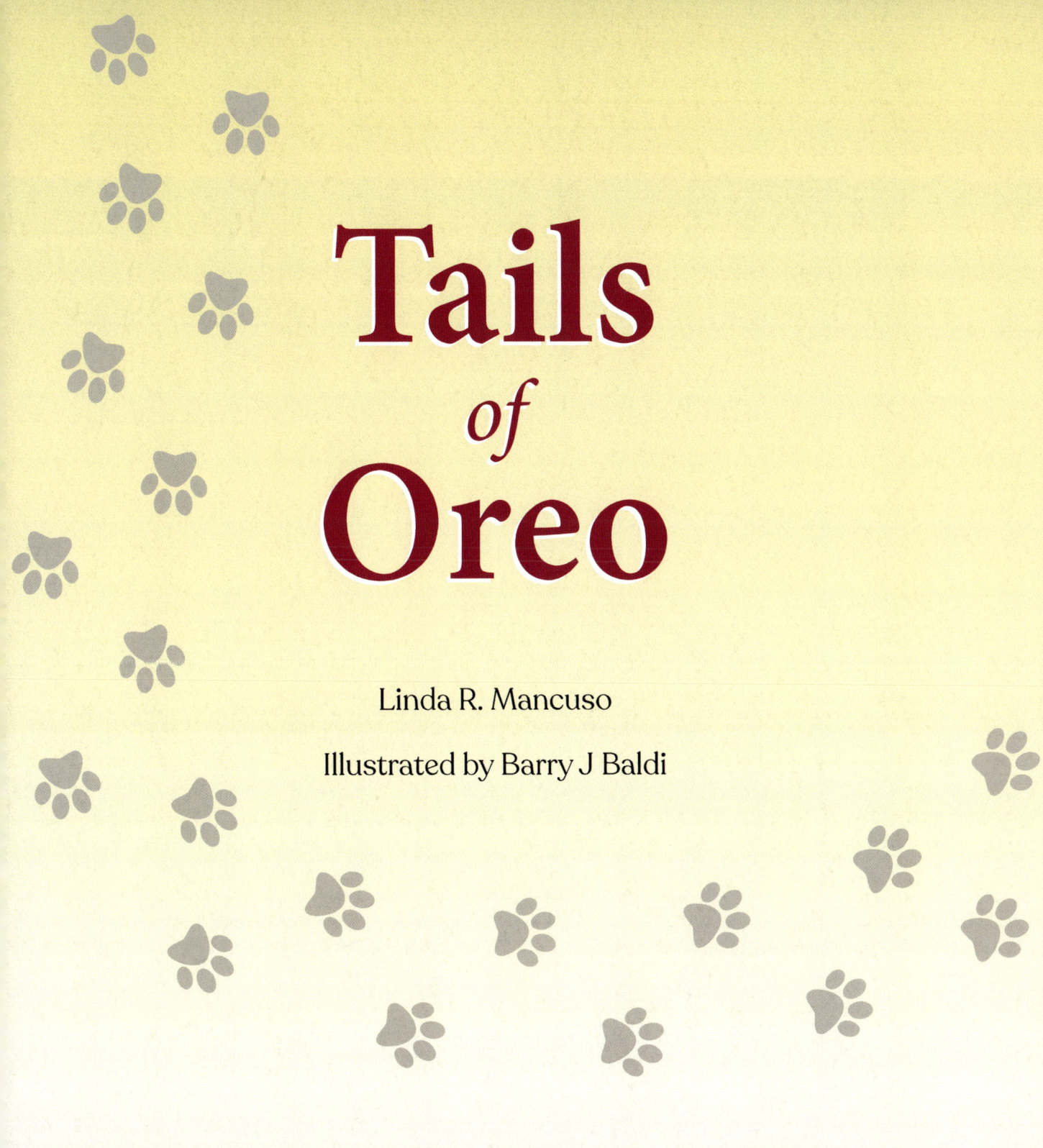

Tails
of
Oreo

Linda R. Mancuso

Illustrated by Barry J Baldi

This Book
is Dedicated to
the Real Oreo,
Who Loves to Play

Once there was a little dog named Oreo.

Oreo was soft and fluffy with colors of brown and tan, and black-tipped ears, a button nose, and his tail curled over his back.

Oreo's fluffy tail caused him a lot of problems on his journey to meet new friends.

And so, the Tails of Oreo...

Oreo loved to chase his tail.
He would go around, round and round, trying to catch his tail.

Oreo would get dizzy trying to chase his tail. He had to stop and lie on his back to stop from spinning.

"Oh!" cried Oreo. "I need friends to play with me."

Oreo wanted to play today, so he went running with his mom. They went up the mountain trail. But Oreo would stop and sniff all the bushes and trees and roll in the dirt.

"Oh! Oh!" cried Oreo. "Something is dragging on my tail!"

"It's just a branch," said Oreo's mom.

But Oreo started running, trying to get the branch off his tail. Around and around in circles ran Oreo as he tried to pull at the branch on his tail.

As Oreo kept circling round and round he got dizzy.
"Wow!" he cried. "I can't stand straight and
I can't stop going around!"

"Oh, no!" screamed Oreo. "Mom! I'm falling!"
Oreo got to the edge of the cliff and started falling.

He landed in a lake... SPLASH!

Up popped Oreo's head from under the water. Splashing and paddling, he saw a row of ducklings swimming in a line behind their mother. "Hey, Ducky!" cried Oreo. "Wait for me! I want to play, too!"

Paddling over to the ducks and getting in line behind the last duckling, Oreo splashed along.

But the mommy duck didn' want Oreo to swim with her ducklings, so she grabbed his tail, scolding him as she pushed him to shore.

So off Oreo went, until he met Mousey.

"Hey, little mouse! You have a long tail too. Can we be friends?" asked Oreo.

But Mousey ran off and hid inside a log.

"Hey, Mousey! Can I come and play inside the log?"

Mousey turned and called to Oreo, "Sure! Come on in."

Oreo was so excited and ran toward the log so fast that he got his tail caught on the edge of the log.

"Oh, no! My tail is hooked on the edge of the log," he cried. "Help me, Mousey!"

Mousey used his sharp fingernails to unhook Oreo's tail, and they both ran inside the log.

"This is fun!" yelled Mousey. "I never had a friend to play inside of my log with me."

Mousey and Oreo stopped
and listened.
They heard a tiny tapping
along the top of the log.
They ran to the end,
and saw a squirrel
running on the log.

"Hey," called Oreo. "You have a long tail
like me and Mousey!
Do you want to play with us?"

"Yes! My name is Raquel,"
said the squirrel.
"Can you climb trees?"

"I can," cried Mousey. "I don't
know if I can," said Oreo.

"Let's go find a tree!"
squealed Raquel.

"Hop on my back,
Mousey!" Oreo said with
a wave of his paw.
"Let's go play
with Raquel!"

Off all three went — Raquel running far in front and Mousey riding on Oreo's back with his straight gray tail curled around Oreo's fluffy tail.

Suddenly, Oreo stopped running and cried, "Look, Mousey! It's a little cat, and he doesn't have a tail."

Oreo and Mousey ran up to the cat.

"Hi! Do you want to play with Mousey, Raquel, and me? My name is Oreo! What is your name?"

"I am Munchins," said the kitty.

"How come you don't have a tail?" asked Oreo. "All cats have long fluffy tails. Mousey has a long straight tail, and I have a curly, fluffy tail. Even Raquel has a long fluffy tail."

Munchins started to cry. "I lost my tail when a mean dog grabbed it."

"Oh! Don't be frightened, Munchins. I am a friendly dog. We will find you a new tail!"

"Yay!" cried Mousey. "It will be long, like mine."

In the meantime, Raquel ran up a tree and yelled down to Oreo and Mousey. "Hey, let's play! Come up into my tree!"

Mousey ran up the tree to meet Raquel.

Oreo barked and jumped.
"I can't get up the tree!"

Oreo stopped and stretched out to rest.

Mousey ran back down the tree and scratched his head.

"Where are we going to find a tail for our friend Munchins?"
Mousey asked.

"How about we all go find a tail for our friend Munchins?" Oreo asked.

"Yes! Let's go!" Raquel ran ahead, jumping on trees and bushes to find a place to get Munchins a tail.

Oreo ran with Mousey on his back.

Munchins ran over rocks and bushes — then they came upon an open meadow.

Suddenly, Oreo stopped running. He saw two tall, yellow ears coming through the grass ahead.

Up popped a bunny, and she hopped over to Oreo, Mousey, Munchins and Raquel.

As she hopped around them, she said, "Hi! I am Binky. Why are you playing in my meadow?"

"We are looking for a tail for Munchins," said Oreo. "He lost it."

Binky turned around and wiggled her round, fuzzy cottontail.
"Everyone doesn't have to have a long tail," she said. "Look at mine!"

"Wow!" cried Oreo. "Gee!" said Mousey.

Munchins ran over to look at Binky's short tail. "I have a short tail
just like you!" Munchins said.

"Yes!" Raquel said. "You *do* have a tail, just a short one!"

They all ran in circles around Munchins —
fluffing, wiggling, and showing off their tails.

"See," said Oreo. "Not everyone has to be the same.
All of us have tails!"

"We just have different-size tails!!" Raquel squealed.

Oreo was so excited to play with his new friends!!!

. . . Oreo stretched out his front paws and yawned.

Opening his eyes and lifting his head from his pillow bed, he saw
all his friends around him.

Ducky, Mousey, Binky, Munchins and Raquel were all resting around Oreo's bed.

"HEY, YOU GUYS! WANT TO PLAY?"

Author • Linda R. Mancuso

Linda Mancuso, born in Almaden Valley, San Jose, California, currently resides in Monterey County.

Linda's professional career has included public relations, media relations, marketing and ownership of three businesses in Santa Clara County. She was very dedicated to community relations in the Silicon Valley with community organizations/events.

In later years, Linda moved to Monterey County to continue her real estate business as a loan signing agent/notary.

Many years of Linda's life have been spent in art and writing. Her passion finally evolved when she joined the Pacific Grove Writers Group, which developed into her decision to write children's books.

Illustrator • Barry J Baldi

A Bay Area native, Barry began his love of drawing and visual storytelling at a young age.

He has expanded those interests to develop his creative skills in a number of media, and pursue a successful career as an illustrator and graphic designer for a variety of clients, publications and personal projects.

Adventurer • Oreo

At six-weeks old, Oreo was drawn to his owner, Linda, upon their first meeting. Oreo's affection and friendliness touched Linda's heart and she realized they were meant to be best friends.

Oreo resides in Monterey County with Linda. They are always seen together whenever they are out, and people stop to pet Oreo or take his photo.